RECLAIM™

LUTHERAN HYMNAL
for CHURCH *and* HOME

Introductory Edition

RECLAIM
RESOURCES

RECLAIM™
Lutheran Hymnal for
Church and Home
Introductory Edition

First printing, June 2006

Copyright © 2006 Reclaim Resources

Except for brief quotations in critical articles or reviews, no part of this book may be reproduced in any manner, printed, electronic, or otherwise, without prior written permission from the publishers or copyright holders. Write to: Permissions, Reclaim Resources, PO Box 8202, Saint Paul, Minn. 55108.

ISBN 1-932458-48-4

For more information on Reclaim Resources, go to www.ReclaimLutheranWorship.org

 Published by Bronze Bow Publishing LLC., 2600 E. 26th Street, Minneapolis, Minn. 55406.

www.bronzebowpublishing.com

This hymnal was designed and set in type by Koechel Peterson and Associates, Inc., Minneapolis, Minn. Hymn engraving by Paul Gerike, Music Advantage, Minneapolis, Minn.

Publication of this book made possible by contributions from many individuals, households, and groups.

Manufactured in the U.S.A.

10 9 8 7 6 5 4 3 2 1

Contents

Introduction 4

Luther's Small Catechism 6
    Introduction 6
    The Ten Commandments 8
    The Creed 10
    The Lord's Prayer 11
    The Sacrament of Baptism 13
    Office of the Keys 14
    Confession of Sin 14
    The Sacrament of the Altar 15
    Household Prayers 16

The Service with Holy Communion 18

Order for Baptism 37

Order for a Wedding 41

Order for a Funeral 44

Hymn Titles and Categories 52

Hymns for Worship 54
   1 Praise to the Lord, the Almighty
   2 Majesty
   3 Holy, Holy, Holy
   4 What a Friend We Have in Jesus
   5 I Was There to Hear Your Borning Cry
   6 O God, Our Help in Ages Past
   7 Nicene Creed
   8 Just as I Am, Without One Plea
   9 Amazing Grace
 10 O Jesus, Blessed Lord to Thee
 11 Lord, with Grateful Hearts
 12 How Great Thou Art
 13 Sunshine and Rain
 14 Now Thank We All Our God
 15 Lord, I Lift Your Name on High
 16 Abide with Me
 17 Nunc Dimittis
 18 Beautiful Savior

Hymns for the Church Year 77
 19 Wake, Awake for Night Is Flying
 20 Joy to the World
 21 Silent Night, Holy Night
 22 Bright and Glorious Is the Sky
 23 In the Cross of Christ I Glory
 24 O Sacred Head, Now Wounded
 25 Beneath the Cross of Jesus
 26 Ah, Holy Jesus
 27 I Know that My Redeemer Lives!
 28 Christ the Lord Is Risen Today!
 29 My Hope Is Built on Nothing Less
 30 O Day Full of Grace
 31 A Mighty Fortress
 32 Children of the Heavenly Father
 33 For All the Saints

Hymns for the Christian Life 96
 34 Just a Closer Walk with Thee
 35 On Eagle's Wings
 36 Great Is Thy Faithfulness
 37 The Church's One Foundation
 38 My Faith Looks Up to Thee
 39 Built on the Rock
 40 Onward, Christian Soldiers
 41 Lord, Keep Us Steadfast in Your Word
 42 I Love to Tell the Story
 43 Softly and Tenderly Jesus Is Calling
 44 Shall We Gather at the River
 45 My God, How Wonderful Thou Art
 46 God's Word Is Our Great Heritage
 47 Rock of Ages, Cleft for Me

What Makes a Hymn Lutheran? 118
A Note on the Liturgical Songs 120
Informal Service 121
Acknowledgments 122
Copyright Information 123
Copyright Holders and Administrators 123
First Lines and Common Titles 124

Introduction

Reclaim, Introductory Edition: Lutheran Hymnal for Church and Home was born out of an awareness that the clarity of Martin Luther's understanding of the worship service was being lost in the pressure to be ecumenical. Over the past century, Lutheran liturgies have come in line with the liturgical revival of the Roman Catholic church. While these efforts to be ecumenical are laudable, Lutherans have left behind Luther's teaching that the center of the Sunday service is about what God has done for us in Jesus Christ, the proclamation of the gospel.

For Lutherans church happens when people gather around the Word. Every service should be proclamation: proclamation from the sermon, from Scripture, and from hymns. When Martin Luther worked on the various orders for the Sunday morning service (the Lord's Supper, baptism, weddings, and funerals), he sought to remove any hint that what we brought to the services, except our repentant hearts, should be celebrated.

Ever since Henry Melchior Muhlenburg, the great American Lutheran patriarch, dreamed that Lutherans in the United States of America could become "one church with one book," Lutherans have tried to realize his dream. The Common Service of 1888 emerged as the evangelical service used by almost all American Lutheran churches. Prepared by a committee of Eastern Lutherans who consulted the best evangelical services of the sixteenth century in Germany, it became the most widely used service among Lutherans in the twentieth century.

To remain faithful to that witness, we have chosen to update the language and music of the Common Service for those Lutherans who desire a faithful evangelical order of service. Thus *Reclaim's* version of the Lord's Supper, or Holy Communion, is cleansed of the eucharistic prayer, as well as any notion of the paschal mystery in which we participate in the death of Christ—and therefore in the atonement. There is no "bringing of the gifts" and no ceremony around the offering. The service does have a clear exhortation to the communicants that both binds and looses the sinner, as per Jesus' command. While the music of worship can be varied, and we intend to offer several musical settings for the liturgy in our complete hymnal, we insist that the words in the liturgy are more important, not the music.

In that same spirit, the *Reclaim* committee has prepared an order for baptism that returns to a clear focus on what Scripture has to say about it. We give little attention to the water of baptism, in line with Luther's Small Catechism, "How can water do such great things? It is not the water, but the word with the water..." We do not include a prayer for the Holy Spirit to come on the one baptized, which reflects a priestly function, but proclaim that the Holy Spirit comes by God's own Word and promise. *Reclaim* has returned the promises of the parents and sponsors to that of raising up children in the Lutheran faith using the Bible and the catechism. *Reclaim* has also restored the solemn promise of the sponsors to see to the spiritual nurture of the child, no matter what happens to the parents.

Likewise, the order for a wedding in *Reclaim* returns to a focus on Scripture and what it has to say to the occasion. It includes a strong emphasis on the love of a man and woman for each other and God, as a way to establish more stable and Christian homes in our midst. Because the service of marriage in *The Book of Common Prayer* is most commonly known and remembered in the English speaking world, we have adapted that service with its traditional vows for our service.

Reclaim's order for a funeral has been restored to the traditional reading of Scripture, especially what is known as the Order of Salvation, so that the living can hear the good news of salvation and be soberly admonished to take care for their own souls. There are no prayers for the dead, no celebration of the life of the deceased, only one place for the eulogy, and a strong urging that the sermon be the gospel of Jesus Christ, not further eulogizing of the dead. These words and hymns are most comforting to mourners who at the time of the funeral are looking for the word of God.

The hymns that we have included in this *Introductory Edition* are among those considered by American Lutherans to be their favorites. The committee added some hymns in order to make the book usable for the complete church year and other occasions. It considers these hymns to be among the most suitable for Lutherans to sing over and over again in their homes and at church so that they learn them. Repetition is how one learns hymns, so we suggest congregations and families use these treasures through the year, repeating them frequently so they can be memorized. We plan to provide a new hymnal with some 600 hymns, but for now these hymns can serve as an anchor to the faith, giving young and old hymns they can sing, by memory, in the face of any joy or sorrow they will meet in their daily lives.

Reclaim, Introductory Edition: Lutheran Hymnal for Church and Home also includes Luther's Small Catechism for teaching in the home and use in the church during the week. It has been the central teaching document of Lutherans over the ages, and it has helped give Lutherans a shelter in the storm of life. It can be used for daily devotions with the family, personal study, and in church on Sunday mornings. With its simple language and pure tone, it is a precious treasure. We can do no better for our children than to teach it to them. We suggest families sing a hymn, read some brief Scripture, repeat a portion of the catechism, and pray one of the prayers of Martin Luther for morning, meals, and evening every day, or as frequently as possible in our busy lives.

Reclaim, Introductory Edition: Lutheran Hymnal for Church and Home is the product of hard work from a committee that took on the task when it appeared that no one else would do so. We are grateful to each member who gave of themselves unstintingly as the project proceeded.

Soli deo Gloria.

Gracia Grindal
Gracia Grindal
Editor-in-Chief

Introduction to Luther's Small Catechism

Dr. Martin Luther was a pastor as well as a monk and a university professor. "Dear God, what misery I beheld," he wrote after touring local churches. "The ordinary person, especially in the villages, knows nothing about the Christian faith. They do not know the Lord's Prayer, the Creed, the Ten Commandments."

Luther took up his pen and began writing single sheets, which sold for a few pennies. These were later collected and published by printers as Luther's "Small Catechism." Each sheet carried the same heading to that particular part of the catechism saying, "...in a simple way in which the head of a household is to present it to a household." Luther thought of a household as a house church. He later wrote, "Every father of a family is a bishop in his house and the wife a bishopess. Therefore, remember that you in your homes are to help us carry on the ministry as we do in the church" (*Luther's Works* 51:137).

Luther envisioned parents at home teaching the central parts of the Christian faith to their children. This makes the father and mother a child's first pastors in fulfilling the Great Commission of "teaching them to observe all that I have commanded you" (Matthew 28:20).

One need not be a theologically trained teacher for this privilege. The very word *catechism* is originally from a Greek word meaning "to repeat back"—a word that by the fourth century was used to describe the basic instruction given to new Christians. It is the way many of us also learned the Lord's Prayer and the Apostles' Creed, saying it along with, or back to, our parents. Luther also wrote "explanations" as well for the Commandments, Creed, and Lord's Prayer, and later added Baptism and the Sacrament of the Altar, making teaching a matter of "repeating back" the answers to "What does this mean?"

Truly we have no greater stewardship as parents and sponsors, than fulfilling our baptismal promises to teach our children the faith. And we have no greater resource for doing it than Luther's Small Catechism.

—Reclaim Committee

The Small Catechism of Dr. Martin Luther

PART I
The Ten Commandments

PART II
The Creed

PART III
The Lord's Prayer

PART IV
The Sacrament of Baptism

PART V
The Sacrament of the Altar

In the plain form in which parents shall teach it to their children and all who live in their home.

PART I
The Ten Commandments

The Introduction
I am the Lord your God.

The First Commandment
You shall have no other gods before me.

What does this mean?

We should fear, love, and trust God above all things.

The Second Commandment
You shall not take the name of the Lord your God in vain; for the Lord will not hold guiltless those who take his name in vain.

What does this mean?

We should fear and love God so that we do not use his name to curse, swear, conjure, lie, or deceive, but call upon him in every time of need, and worship him with prayer, praise, and thanksgiving.

The Third Commandment
Remember the Sabbath day, to keep it holy.

What does this mean?

We should fear and love God so that we do not despise his Word and the preaching of it, but recognize that it is holy, and gladly hear and learn it.

The Fourth Commandment
Honor your father and your mother, that your days may be long in the land which the Lord your God is giving you.

What does this mean?

We should fear and love God so that we do not show contempt for our parents and superiors, nor provoke them to anger, but honor, serve, obey, love, and esteem them.

The Fifth Commandment
You shall not kill.

What does this mean?

We should fear and love God so that we do our neighbors no bodily harm nor cause them any suffering, but help and befriend them in every need.

The Sixth Commandment
You shall not commit adultery.

What does this mean?

We should fear and love God so that we lead a chaste and pure life in word and deed, and that husband and wife love and honor each other.

The Seventh Commandment
You shall not steal.

What does this mean?

We should fear and love God so that we do not rob our neighbors of their money or property, nor take from them by unfair dealing or fraud, but help them to improve and protect their property and means of making a living.

The Eighth Commandment

You shall not bear false witness against your neighbor.

What does this mean?

We should fear and love God so that we do not deceitfully lie, betray, gossip about, or slander our neighbors, but defend them, speak well of them, and put the most charitable construction on all that they do.

The Ninth Commandment

You shall not covet your neighbor's house.

What does this mean?

We should fear and love God so that we do not plot to take our neighbors' possessions, inheritance, or home, nor obtain them under pretense of a legal right, but assist and serve our neighbors in keeping what is theirs.

The Tenth Commandment

You shall not covet your neighbor's wife, or his manservant, or his maidservant, or his cattle, or anything that is your neighbor's.

What does this mean?

We should fear and love God so that we do not cause alienation among our neighbor's wife, servants, or cattle, or try to lure them away, but encourage them to remain and serve him faithfully.

The Conclusion

What does God declare concerning all these commandments? He says: I the Lord your God am a jealous God, visiting the wickedness of the fathers upon the children to the third and fourth generation of those who hate me but showing mercy unto thousands of those who love me and keep my commandments.

What does this mean?

God threatens to punish all who violate these commandments. We should, therefore, fear his anger and in no way disobey them. But God promises grace and every blessing to all who keep these commandments. We should, therefore, love him, trust in him, and gladly keep his commandments.

PART II
The Creed

The First Article—Creation
I believe in God, the Father Almighty, creator of heaven and earth.

What does this mean?

I believe that God has created me and all that exists. He has given me and still preserves my body and soul, my eyes and ears, my reason and all my senses, together with food and clothing, home and family, and all my property. Every day, he provides abundantly for all the needs of my life, protects me from all danger, and guards and keeps me from all evil. He does this purely out of fatherly and divine goodness and mercy, though I do not deserve nor am I worthy of it. Therefore, I ought to thank, praise, serve, and obey him. This is most certainly true.

The Second Article—Redemption
I believe in Jesus Christ, his only Son, our Lord. He was conceived by the power of the Holy Spirit and born of the Virgin Mary. He suffered under Pontius Pilate, was crucified, died, and was buried. He descended into hell. On the third day he rose again. He ascended into heaven, and is seated at the right hand of the Father. He will come again to judge the living and the dead.

What does this mean?

I believe that Jesus Christ, true God, begotten of the Father from eternity, and also true man, born of the Virgin Mary, is my Lord. He has redeemed me, a lost and condemned creature, bought and freed me from all sins, from death, and from the power of the devil, not with silver and gold, but with his holy and precious blood and his innocent suffering and death. He does all this in order that I might be his own, live under him in his kingdom, and serve him in everlasting righteousness, innocence, and blessedness, even as he is risen from the dead, and lives and reigns for all eternity. This is most certainly true.

The Third Article—Sanctification
I believe in the Holy Spirit, the holy Christian church, the communion of saints, the forgiveness of sins, the resurrection of the body, and the life everlasting. Amen.

What does this mean?

I believe that I cannot by my own reason or strength believe in Jesus Christ, my Lord, or come to him; but the Holy Spirit has called me through the Gospel, enlightened me with his gifts, and sanctified and preserved me in the true faith. In the same way, he calls, gathers, enlightens, and sanctifies the whole Christian church on earth, and preserves it in unity with Jesus Christ in the one true faith. In this Christian church, he daily forgives abundantly all my sins, and the sins of all believers, and at the last day will raise me and all the dead, and will grant everlasting life to me and to all who believe in Christ. This is most certainly true.

PART III
The Lord's Prayer

The Introduction
Our Father who art in heaven.

What does this mean?

God here tenderly encourages us to believe that he is truly our Father, and that we are truly his children, so that we may boldly and confidently pray to him, just as beloved children speak to their dear father.

The First Petition
Hallowed be thy name.

What does this mean?

God's name is indeed holy in itself, but we pray in this petition that it may be kept holy also among us.

How is this done?

God's name is hallowed when his word is taught in its truth and purity, and we, as God's children, lead holy lives in accordance with it. Grant this to us, dear Father in heaven! But whoever teaches and lives in ways other than what God's word teaches desecrates the name of God among us. Prevent us from doing this, heavenly Father!

The Second Petition
Thy kingdom come.

What does this mean?

The kingdom of God comes indeed by itself, without our prayer, but we pray in this petition that it may also come to us.

How is this done?

God's kingdom comes when our heavenly Father gives us his Holy Spirit, so that by his grace we believe his holy word and live a godly life here on earth and in heaven forever.

The Third Petition
Thy will be done, on earth as it is in heaven.

What does this mean?

The good and gracious will of God is done indeed without our prayer, but we pray in this petition that it may also be done among us.

How is this done?

God's will is done when he destroys and makes futile every evil design and purpose of the devil, the world, and our own flesh that would keep us from hallowing his name and prevent the coming of his kingdom, and when he strengthens us and keeps us steadfast in his word and in faith throughout our lives. This is his good and gracious will.

The Fourth Petition
Give us this day our daily bread.

What does this mean?

God indeed gives daily bread to all people, even the wicked, without our prayer, but we pray in this petition that he would lead us to recognize that our daily bread comes from him as a gift and to receive it with thanksgiving.

What is meant by daily bread?

Daily bread means everything that is required to meet our earthly needs, such as food, clothing, and housing; employment, money, and necessities; devout parents, children, and communities; godly and faithful authorities, good government, seasonable weather, peace and health, an orderly society and a good reputation, true friends, good neighbors, and the like.

The Fifth Petition
And forgive us our trespasses, as we forgive those who trespass against us.

What does this mean?

We pray in this petition that our heavenly Father would not regard our sins or deny our prayers because of them—for we have not earned nor do we deserve those things for which we pray—but that he would grant us all things through grace, even though we sin every day and deserve nothing but punishment. And certainly we, too, will heartily forgive, and gladly do good to those who sin against us.

The Sixth Petition
And lead us not into temptation.

What does this mean?

God indeed tempts no one to sin, but we pray in this petition that God would so guard and protect us that the devil, the world, and our own flesh may not deceive us or lead us into false belief, despair, and other great and shameful sins, but that when tempted in such ways, we may finally prevail and gain the victory.

The Seventh Petition
But deliver us from evil.

What does this mean?

We pray in this petition, as in a summary, that our heavenly Father would deliver us from every type of evil—whether it affect body or soul, property or reputation—and at last, when the hour of death comes, would grant us a blessed end, and graciously take us from this world of sorrow to himself in heaven.

The Conclusion
For thine is the kingdom, and the power, and the glory, forever and ever. Amen.

What does this mean?

It means that I should be certain that such petitions are acceptable to our heavenly Father and are heard by him, for he himself has commanded us to pray in this manner and has promised to hear us. "Amen, amen" means "Yes, yes, it shall be so."

PART IV
The Sacrament of Baptism

What is baptism?

Baptism is not merely water, but it is water used according to God's command and connected with God's word.

What is this word of God?

It is the word of our Lord Jesus Christ, as recorded in the last chapter of Matthew: "Go therefore and make disciples of all the nations, baptizing them in the name of the Father, and of the Son, and of the Holy Spirit."

What gifts or benefits does baptism bring?

It works forgiveness of sins, delivers from death and the devil, and gives everlasting salvation to all who believe, as the word and promise of God declare.

What is this word and promise of God?

It is the word of our Lord Jesus Christ, as recorded in the last chapter of Mark, "Whoever believes and is baptized will be saved, but whoever does not believe will be condemned" (Mark 16:16).

How can water do such great things?

It is not the water that does these things, but the word of God connected with the water and our faith which relies on that word of God. For without the word of God, it is simply water and not baptism. But when connected with the word of God, it is a baptism, that is, a gracious water of life and a washing of regeneration in the Holy Spirit. As Saint Paul says to Titus, "He saved us, not because of works done by us in righteousness, but according to his own mercy, by the washing of regeneration and renewal of the Holy Spirit, whom he poured out on us richly through Jesus Christ our Savior, so that being justified by his grace we might become heirs according to the hope of eternal life" (Titus 3:5-8). This is most certainly true.

What is the significance of such baptizing with water?

It signifies that the old Adam in us, together with all sins and evil desires, should be drowned by daily sorrow for sin and repentance and be put to death, and that the new person should come forth every day and rise to live before God in righteousness and holiness for ever.

Where is it so written?

Saint Paul says in Romans, "We were buried therefore with him by baptism into death, in order that, just as Christ was raised from the dead by the glory of the Father, we too might walk in newness of life" (Romans 6:4).

OFFICE OF THE KEYS

What is the Office of the Keys?

It is the unique power which Christ has given to his church on earth to forgive the sins of penitent sinners, and to retain the sins of the impenitent, so long as they do not repent.

"If you forgive the sins of anyone, they are forgiven; if you withhold forgiveness from anyone, it is withheld" (John 20:23).

"Truly, I say to you, whatever you bind on earth shall be bound in heaven, and whatever you loose on earth shall be loosed in heaven" (Matthew 18:18).

CONFESSION OF SIN

We have a good tool to use in our life: confession. We can use this tool by speaking privately to another person and by speaking together in the assembly of believers. When we confess in confidence to another (normally to a pastor), we can have the joy and relief of stating to this trusted person what deeply troubles us, and from that person hearing, as from Christ himself, words of forgiveness and assurance. In this way also, Christ works to confront us in our sin and free us from its disabling power.

— Reclaim Committee

What is confession?

Confession consists of two parts. One is that we confess our sins and the other is that we receive absolution, or forgiveness, from the confessor as from God himself, in no way doubting, but firmly believing that our sins are thereby forgiven before God in heaven.

What sins should we confess?

Before God we should acknowledge ourselves guilty of all kinds of sins, even those of which we are not aware, as we do in the Lord's Prayer. To the confessor, however, we should confess only those sins which we know and which trouble us.

What are such sins?

Here examine yourself in the light of the Ten Commandments whether as father or mother, son or daughter, employer or employee, you have been disobedient, unfaithful, lazy, angry, sexually unfaithful, or quarrelsome; whether you have injured anyone by word or deed; stolen, neglected, or wasted anything; or done any other evil.

PART V
The Sacrament of the Altar

What is the Sacrament of the Altar?

It is the true body and blood of our Lord Jesus Christ, under the bread and wine, given to us Christians to eat and drink, as it was instituted by Christ himself.

Where is it so written?

Our Lord Jesus Christ, on the night in which he was betrayed, took bread; and when he had given thanks, he broke it and gave it to his disciples saying: Take, eat, this is my body, which is given for you; do this in remembrance of me.

Again, after supper he took the cup, gave thanks, and gave it to them saying: Take, and drink of it, all of you. This cup is the new testament in my blood, which is shed for you and for many for the forgiveness of sins. Do this, as often as you drink it, in remembrance of me.

What is the benefit of such eating and drinking?

It is pointed out in these words: "Given and shed for you for the forgiveness of sins." Through these words the forgiveness of sin, life, and salvation are given to us in the sacrament; for where there is forgiveness of sin, there is also life and salvation.

How can the bodily eating and drinking produce such great benefits?

The eating and drinking certainly do not produce them, but the words, "Given and shed for you for the forgiveness of sins." These words, together with the eating and drinking, are the chief thing in the sacrament and those who believe them have what they say and declare, namely, the forgiveness of sins.

Who, then, receives the sacrament worthily?

Fasting and bodily preparation are indeed a good outward discipline, but they are truly worthy and well prepared who believe these words, "Given and shed for you for the forgiveness of sins." But those who do not believe these words or who doubt them are unworthy and unprepared, for the words, "For you," require truly believing hearts.

HOUSEHOLD PRAYERS

How the head of the family is to teach members of the household to say morning and evening prayers.

A Morning Prayer

In the morning, when you get out of bed, make the sign of the cross and say, "In the name of the Father, and of the Son, and of the Holy Spirit."

Then, finding a comfortable place, say the Apostles' Creed and the Lord's Prayer.

You may also use this prayer:

> I thank you, my heavenly Father, through Jesus Christ, your dear Son, that you have kept me this night from all harm and danger; and I ask you to protect me this day also from sin and every evil, that in all I do today I may please you. For into your hands I commend myself, my body and soul, and all that is mine. Let your holy angel watch over me, that the wicked foe have no power over me. Amen.

After singing or reading a hymn, or according to your devotional habits, you are to go to your work with confidence and joy.

An Evening Prayer

In the evening, before you go to bed, make the sign of the cross and say: "In the Name of the Father, and of the Son, and of the Holy Spirit. Amen."

Then, finding a comfortable place, say the Apostles' Creed and the Lord's Prayer. You may also use this prayer:

> I thank you, heavenly Father, through Jesus Christ, your dear Son, that you have graciously protected me today; and I ask you to forgive me all my sins and the wrong which I have done. By your mercy, graciously protect me from the dangers of this night. Into your hands I commend myself, my body and soul, and all that is mine. Let your holy angel watch over me, that the wicked foe have no power over me. Amen.

Then you are to lie down in peace and sleep.

Prayer before Eating

When children and all members of the household gather at the table, they are to reverently fold their hands and pray:

> The eyes of all wait upon you, O Lord, and you give them their food in due season. You open your hand and satisfy the desire of every living thing.

Then they are to pray the Lord's Prayer and the following prayer:

> Lord God, heavenly Father, bless us and these your gifts, which we receive from your bountiful goodness, through Jesus Christ, our Lord. Amen.

Prayer after Eating

After eating, also, they should fold their hands and devoutly pray:

> Oh, give thanks to the Lord, for he is good, and his mercy endures forever. He gives to the beasts their food, and to the young ravens that cry. His delight is not in the strength of the horse, nor is he impressed by the speed of an athlete. Instead, the Lord takes pleasure in those who fear him, in those who hope in his steadfast love.

Then say the Lord's Prayer followed by this prayer:

> We thank you, Lord God, heavenly Father, through Jesus Christ, our Lord, for all your benefits. You live and reign forever and ever. Amen.

The Service with Holy Communion
Saint Paul's Setting

In the name of the Father, and of the ✠ Son, and of the Holy Spirit.
Amen.

CONFESSION OF SIN

Beloved in the Lord! Let us draw near with a true heart, and confess our sin to God our Father, imploring him, in the name of our Lord Jesus Christ, to grant us forgiveness.

Our help is in the name of the Lord.
Who made heaven and earth.

I said, I will confess my transgressions to the Lord.
And you forgave the iniquity of my sin.

Almighty God, our Maker and Redeemer, we poor sinners confess to you that we are by nature sinful and unclean, and that we have sinned against you in thought, word, and deed. Therefore we flee for refuge to your infinite mercy, seeking and imploring your grace, for the sake of your Son, Jesus Christ our Lord.

Most merciful God, you have given your only Son to die for us. Have mercy on us, and for his sake grant us remission of all our sins. By your Holy Spirit increase in us true knowledge of you and of your will, and true obedience to your word, so that by your grace we may come to everlasting life; through Jesus Christ our Lord. Amen.

ABSOLUTION

Almighty God, our heavenly Father, has had mercy on you, and has given his only Son to die for you, and for his sake forgives you all your sins. Scripture declares: Whoever believes in the Son has eternal life; whoever does not, shall not see life. Therefore God continues to call the unbelieving to turn from their impenitence while it is day, and come to repentance and faith in Jesus Christ. For to all who receive him and who believe in his name, he gives power to become children of God, and bestows on them the Holy Spirit. All who believe and are baptized will be saved.
Amen.

— OR —

Almighty God, our heavenly Father, has had mercy on you, and has given his only Son to die for you, and for his sake forgives you all your sins. To all who believe in Jesus Christ he gives the power to become children of God, and bestows on you his Holy Spirit. On the other hand, I declare to the impenitent and unbelieving, that so long as you continue in your impenitence, God has not forgiven your sins, and will surely visit your iniquities upon you if you do not turn from your sinful ways and come to repentance and faith in Christ before the day of grace is ended.
Amen.

HYMN

KYRIE ELEISON

© 2006 John C. Ylvisaker

THE SERVICE WITH HOLY COMMUNION

GLORIA IN EXCELSIS

Cantor: Glo-ry be to God on high and on earth peace, good will to all.

1 Lord, we praise your name on high, wor-ship you and glo-ri-fy.
2 You have borne the sins of all. Mer-cy, Lord, and hear our call.
3 You, a-lone, the Ho-ly One, You, a-lone, God's on-ly Son,

To the Lamb of God we cry and join the an-gel's song.
Ev-'ry-one, both great and small, come join the an-gel's song.
In your name we've just be-gun to join the an-gel's song.

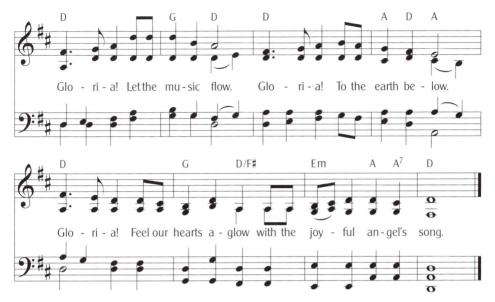

© 2006 John C. Ylvisaker

The Lord be with you.
And with your spirit.

PRAYER OF THE DAY

Let us pray.

The minister prays the Prayer of the Day.

Amen.

FIRST LESSON

The First Lesson is written in the _____ chapter of _____.

After the Lesson the reader may say, "The word of the Lord."

PSALM OR ANTHEM

SECOND LESSON

The Second Lesson is written in the _____ chapter of _____.

After the Lesson the reader may say, "The word of the Lord."

Stand

THE SERVICE WITH HOLY COMMUNION

HALLELUJAH

Hal-le-lu! Hal-le-lu-jah! Give praise to the Lord for the blessings of heaven in God's holy Word. For the words of forgiveness, the words that endure, (hal-le-lu! hal-le-lu-jah!) give praise to the Lord.

Text © 2006 John C. Ylvisaker

THE SERVICE WITH HOLY COMMUNION

— OR —

LENTEN SENTENCE

Text © 2006 John C. Ylvisaker

GOSPEL

The Gospel is written in the _____ chapter of _____ .

Glory be to you, O Lord.

After the Gospel the reader may say, "The Gospel of the Lord."

Praise be to you, O Christ.

THE APOSTLES' CREED

**I believe in God, the Father almighty,
  creator of heaven and earth.**

**I believe in Jesus Christ, his only Son, our Lord.
  He was conceived by the power of the Holy Spirit
    and born of the Virgin Mary,
  He suffered under Pontius Pilate,
    was crucified, died, and was buried.
  He descended into hell.
  On the third day he rose again.
  He ascended into heaven,
    and is seated at the right hand of the Father.
  He will come again to judge the living and the dead.**

**I believe in the Holy Spirit,
  the holy Christian church,
  the communion of saints,
  the forgiveness of sins,
  the resurrection of the body,
  and the life everlasting. Amen.**

— OR —

The Nicene Creed may be said or sung (see Hymn 7). It is used on Festivals or when Baptism or Holy Communion is administered.

THE NICENE CREED

We believe in one God,
  the Father, the Almighty,
  maker of heaven and earth,
  of all that is, seen and unseen.

We believe in one Lord, Jesus Christ,
  the only Son of God,
  eternally begotten of the Father,
  God from God, Light from Light,
  true God from true God,
  begotten, not made,
  of one Being with the Father.
  Through him all things were made.
  For us and for our salvation
    he came down from heaven;
    by the power of the Holy Spirit
      he became incarnate from the Virgin Mary, and was made man.
  For our sake he was crucified under Pontius Pilate;
    he suffered death and was buried.
    On the third day he rose again
      in accordance with the Scriptures;
    he ascended into heaven
      and is seated at the right hand of the Father.
  He will come again in glory to judge the living and the dead,
  and his kingdom will have no end.

We believe in the Holy Spirit, the Lord, the giver of life,
  who proceeds from the Father and the Son.
  With the Father and the Son he is worshiped and glorified.
  He has spoken through the prophets.
  We believe in one holy Christian and apostolic church.
  We acknowledge one Baptism for the forgiveness of sins.
  We look for the resurrection of the dead,
    and the life of the world to come. Amen.

Sit

THE SERVICE WITH HOLY COMMUNION

HYMN

SERMON

The peace of God, which passes all understanding, keep your hearts and minds through Christ Jesus unto life everlasting.
Amen.

HYMN

During the hymn, gifts and tithes are received and may be placed on the altar by the ushers.

ANNOUNCEMENTS

Here may follow orders for baptism, confirmation, ordination, wedding, installation, and dedication.

PRAYER OF THE CHURCH

Almighty and merciful God, the Father of our Lord Jesus Christ, we thank you for your continual goodness and tender mercies, especially in sending your Son, Jesus Christ our Lord, as the revelation of your saving grace and truth, your living, incarnate Word. We pray that Christ may so dwell in our hearts through faith that we may be filled with his endless life and daily abound in his redeeming work. Lord in your mercy,
hear our prayer.

We pray for your holy church; defend and preserve it in the truth of your Word. Continue to send your Word and Holy Spirit throughout the world calling, gathering, and enlightening your whole church, and preserving it in union with Jesus Christ in the one true faith. So that your light and truth may reach to the uttermost parts of the earth, raise up faithful pastors and messengers, and embolden Christians everywhere to be faithful witnesses, trusting that your Word, like the rain, will never return to you void, but will accomplish that for which you sent it. Lord, in your mercy,
hear our prayer.

Let the light of your Word shine in our homes. Enable and empower parents to teach their children by word and example the daily life of believers. Bless all centers of learning and all who administer and teach in them, that they may send forth men and women committed to serving you. And grant that they may look to you, as the fountain of all wisdom. For all to whom we entrust the authority to govern; we ask for wisdom, guidance, and strength. Help them to

THE SERVICE WITH HOLY COMMUNION

serve your purposes and establish good order, peace, justice, and prosperity for the common good. Cause the earth to yield its fruit in its season and make us responsible stewards of our resources. Give success to all beneficial occupations, to all true art and useful knowledge, and crown all such endeavors with your blessing. Lord, in your mercy,
hear our prayer.

For all who are in trouble, want, sickness, adversity, or peril of death, especially those who suffer persecution for your name's sake: grant them strength and peace within, to endure the buffeting of body and soul in the confidence that they are always in your keeping, and nothing can ever snatch them out of their Father's hands. Most gracious Father, although we deserve the just consequences of our sins, we pray that you would graciously defend us from all harm. Protect us from false and pernicious influences in the world, from violence and immorality, pornography and lewdness, from plagues and disease, from famine and terror, and most of all from unbelief and despair of your mercy. In all our temptations and needs help us to turn and to trust in you as our very present help in trouble. Lord, in your mercy,
hear our prayer.

Here special supplications, intercessions, and prayers may be made.

Lord, be merciful to all, and when we reach our final hour, grant us a blessed departure from this world, and on the last day, a resurrection into your glory.
Amen.

– OR –

Almighty God, the Father of our Lord Jesus Christ:

We pray for your holy church gathered and nurtured by your Word and sent into the world to be the body of Christ. Give us always the mind of Christ, that we may seek the lost, bring good news to the afflicted, bind up the broken hearted, and proclaim liberty to the captive. Empower us for mission with purity in teaching, holiness in living, and Christ likeness in serving. Lord, in your mercy,
hear our prayer.

We pray for all to whom we entrust authority to govern. Help them to serve according to your will so that mercy and truth, justice and peace may prevail. Lord, in your mercy,
hear our prayer.

We pray for all who suffer sickness, sorrow, and adversity. We pray especially for ____*Name*____ and for those whom we name in our hearts before you.

Make bold all who are persecuted for righteousness' sake. Keep safe those who endanger their lives protecting others. Refresh those who bear heavy burdens; and use us as messengers of your mercy and instruments of your peace. Lord, in your mercy,
hear our prayer.

Lord, be merciful to all, and when we reach our final hour, grant us a blessed departure from this world, and on the last day, a resurrection into your glory. **Amen.**

If there be no Holy Communion, the service concludes with the Lord's Prayer, Hymn, and Benediction.

LORD'S PRAYER

Our Father, who art in heaven,
  hallowed be thy name,
  thy kingdom come,
  thy will be done,
    on earth as it is in heaven.
Give us this day our daily bread;
and forgive us our trespasses,
  as we forgive those
    who trespass against us;
and lead us not into temptation,
  but deliver us from evil.
For thine is the kingdom,
  and the power, and the glory,
  forever and ever. Amen.

HYMN

The Benediction may be said or sung (see page 36).

BENEDICTION

The Lord bless you, and keep you,
The Lord make his face shine upon you, and be gracious unto you.
The Lord lift up his countenance upon you, and ✚ give you peace.

HOLY COMMUNION

When there is Communion, the bread and wine are prepared during the singing of the Hymn.

HYMN

Stand

EXHORTATION — OR —

Brothers and sisters in Christ, to receive this Holy Sacrament in a worthy manner, consider what we must now believe and do.

We should believe that Jesus Christ himself is truly present in the bread and wine as his words declare: This is my body, which is given for you; this is my blood, which is shed for you for the forgiveness of sin.

We should also trust that Jesus Christ forgives our sins as his words promise: for the forgiveness of sin.

Finally, we should do as Christ commands when he says: Take. Eat. Drink. Do this in remembrance of me.

When we repent, believe these words, and do as Christ commands, then we have rightly examined ourselves and may worthily come to the Lord's table for the forgiveness of all our sins.

Together, we should also give thanks to the Father of our Lord Jesus Christ for this great gift. We should love one another with a pure heart, and with the whole Christian church take comfort and joy in Christ our Lord. May our heavenly Father grant us his grace; through our Lord Jesus Christ. Amen.

Brothers and sisters in Christ, the Apostle Paul admonishes us: Examine yourselves before eating the bread and drinking the cup.

Scripture hereby encourages us to come to the Lord's table, believing that Jesus Christ is himself present in the bread and the wine as his words declare: This is my body. This is my blood.

Scripture also encourages us to come trusting in the forgiveness of sins, as Jesus says, "For you, for the forgiveness of sin."

Finally we are encouraged to do as Christ commands when he says: Take. Eat. Drink. Do this in remembrance of me.

When we repent of sin, believe his words, and do as he commands, we come in a worthy manner, and join the whole Christian church on earth in giving thanks to God the Father of our Lord Jesus Christ for so great a gift. We also pray that his love will renew our love for one another and that we, with the whole Christian church, may know the comfort and joy that is in Christ our Savior and Lord. Receive now his grace with believing hearts. Amen.

THE SERVICE WITH HOLY COMMUNION

PREFACE

The Lord be with you.
And with your spirit.

Lift up your hearts.
We lift them to the Lord.

Let us give thanks to the Lord our God.
It is right to give him thanks and praise.

It is truly good, right, and salutary, that we should at all times, and in all places, give thanks to you, O Lord, holy Father, almighty everlasting God:

PROPER PREFACES

Advent

Through Jesus Christ our Lord, whom John the baptizer heralded as the anointed One, the very Lamb of God, calling sinners to repent, to escape the judgment of his coming. Therefore with angels…

Christmas

For in the mystery of the Word made flesh, you have given us a new revelation of your glory; that seeing you in the person of your Son, we may be drawn to the love of those things which are not seen. Therefore with angels…

Epiphany

And now we praise you, that you have sent to us your only begotten Son, and that in him, being found in the form of a man, you have revealed the fullness of your Glory. Therefore with angels…

Lent

You call your people to repent of sin and prepare for the joy of the paschal feast. Renew us in faith and holiness, and bring us into the fullness of your grace and truth that belongs to the children of God. Therefore with angels…

Holy Week

Who on the tree of the cross gave salvation to humankind; so when death arose, life also might rise again. And that the serpent who by a tree once overcame, might likewise by a tree be overcome, through Christ our Lord. Therefore with angels…

Easter

But chiefly are we bound to praise you for the glorious resurrection of your Son, Jesus Christ, our Lord. For he is the very Paschal Lamb, who was offered for us, and has taken away the sin of the world. Who by his death has destroyed death, and by his rising to life again, has restored to us everlasting life. Therefore with angels...

Ascension

Through Jesus Christ our Lord. Who after his Resurrection appeared openly to all his disciples, and in their sight was taken up into Heaven, that he might make us partakers of his Divine Nature. Therefore with angels...

Pentecost (and the Sundays in Pentecost)

Through Jesus Christ, your dear Son, our Lord and Savior, who ascending above the heavens and sitting at your right hand, poured out [on this day] the Holy Spirit as he had promised upon the chosen disciples; therefore the whole earth rejoices with great joy. Therefore with angels...

Trinity

Who with your only-begotten Son, and the Holy Spirit, are one God, one Lord. And in the confession of the only true God, we worship the Trinity in person, and the unity in substance, of majesty co-equal. Therefore with angels...

All Saints

Who did surround us with so great a cloud of witnesses, to encourage us with their fellowship to run the race that is set before us; and with them to obtain the everlasting crown. Therefore with angels...

...*Therefore with angels and archangels*, and with all the company of heaven, we laud and magnify your glorious name; evermore praising you, and saying:

THE SERVICE WITH HOLY COMMUNION

SANCTUS

© 2006 John C. Ylvisaker

LORD'S PRAYER

**Our Father, who art in heaven,
 hallowed be thy name,
 thy kingdom come,
 thy will be done,
  on earth as it is in heaven.
Give us this day our daily bread;
and forgive us our trespasses,
 as we forgive those
  who trespass against us;
and lead us not into temptation,
 but deliver us from evil.
For thine is the kingdom,
 and the power, and the glory,
 forever and ever. Amen.**

WORDS OF INSTITUTION

Our Lord Jesus Christ, on the night in which he was betrayed, took bread; and when he had given thanks, he broke it and gave it to his disciples saying: Take, eat, this is my body, which is given for you; do this in remembrance of me.

Again, after supper he took the cup, gave thanks, and gave it to them saying: Take, and drink of it, all of you. This cup is the new testament in my blood, which is shed for you and for many for the forgiveness of sins. Do this, as often as you drink it, in remembrance of me.

THE SERVICE WITH HOLY COMMUNION

AGNUS DEI

Lamb of God, you take the sins of the world. Lamb of God, your mercies never cease. Lamb of God, you take the sins of the world. Jesus Christ, Lamb of God, O won't you give us peace.

© 2006 John C. Ylvisaker

As the ministers distribute the bread and wine, they say these words to each communicant:

The body of Christ.

The blood of Christ.

The presiding minister and assisting ministers commune after the congregation.

The body of our Lord Jesus Christ and his precious blood strengthen and preserve you in true faith to everlasting life.

The Nunc Dimittis may be said or sung (see Hymn 17).

NUNC DIMITTIS

Lord, now let your servant depart in peace,
  according to your word.
For my eyes have seen your salvation,
  which you have prepared before the face of all people:
A light to lighten the Gentiles
  and the glory of your people Israel.
Glory be to the Father, and to the Son,
  and to the Holy Spirit,
As it was in the beginning, is now, and ever shall be,
  world without end. Amen.

THANKSGIVING

We give you thanks, almighty God, that you have refreshed us through this your salutary gift; and we ask you in your mercy to strengthen us through the same in faith toward you and in fervent love toward one another; through Jesus Christ, your dear Son, our Lord, who lives and reigns with you and the Holy Spirit, one God, world without end.
Amen.

BENEDICAMUS

The Lord be with you.
And with your spirit.

Bless the Lord.
Thanks be to God.

Stand

The Benediction may be said or sung (see page 36)

BENEDICTION

The Lord bless you, and keep you,
The Lord make his face shine upon you, and be gracious unto you.
The Lord lift up his countenance upon you, and ✞ give you peace.

Amen.

—OR—

THE SERVICE WITH HOLY COMMUNION

AARON'S BENEDICTION

1 O Lord, bless and keep us all. O Lord, bless and keep us all. O Lord, bless and keep us all. Bless ev-'ry-one, great and small.
2 O Lord, make your face to shine. O Lord, make your face to shine. O Lord, make your face to shine. Be gra-cious and keep us thine.
3 O Lord, lift your eyes to see. O Lord, lift your eyes to see. O Lord, lift your eyes to see The peace that we need from thee.

Text © 2006 John C. Ylvisaker

Order for Holy Baptism

May be used at a public service.

A hymn may be sung.

In the name of the Father, and of the ✢ Son, and of the Holy Spirit. Amen.

Dear Friends in Christ,
All people are born in sin. Our Savior Jesus Christ has said, "No one can see the kingdom of God without being born again" (see John 3:3). Let us call upon God, the Father of our Lord Jesus Christ, that in his goodness and mercy, he will receive ____Name____ by baptism and make ____Name____ a member of his holy church.

Let us pray.
Almighty and everlasting God, the Father of our Lord Jesus Christ, by whose power we are born again: Grant to all those who seek the gift of Holy Baptism, your everlasting grace by the washing of regeneration (Titus 3:5). Receive them, O Lord, as you have promised, through your beloved Son saying, "Ask and it will be given to you; seek and you will find; knock and it will be opened to you" (Matthew 7:7), through the same, Jesus Christ, your Son our Lord. Amen.

> *For the baptism of children.*
>
> Let us hear the Holy Gospel.
>
> "And they were bringing children to him that he might touch them, and the disciples rebuked them. But when Jesus saw it, he was indignant and said to them, 'Let the children come to me; do not hinder them, for to such belongs the kingdom of God. Truly, I say to you, whoever does not receive the kingdom of God like a child shall not enter it.' And he took them in his arms and blessed them, laying his hands on them" (Mark 10:13-16).

Our risen Lord Jesus Christ said, "All authority in heaven and on earth has been given to me. Go therefore and make disciples of all nations, baptizing them in the name of the Father and of the Son and of the Holy Spirit, teaching them to observe all that I have commanded you; and behold, I am with you always, to the end of the age" (Matthew 28:18-20).

ORDER FOR HOLY BAPTISM

LORD'S PRAYER

**Our Father, who art in heaven,
 hallowed by thy name,
 thy kingdom come,
 thy will be done,
  on earth as it is in heaven.
Give us this day our daily bread;
and forgive us our trespasses,
 as we forgive those
  who trespass against us;
and lead us not into temptation,
 but deliver us from evil.
For thine is the kingdom,
 and the power, and the glory,
 forever and ever. Amen.**

✝ *For the baptism of children.*

Then shall the minister say to those who present the child.

In obedience to our Lord's command, you bring this child for Holy Baptism. I therefore ask you:

✝ *For the baptism of adults.*

_____Name_____, I ask you:

Do you renounce the devil and all his works and ways?
Response: I renounce them.

Do you believe in God the Father almighty, creator of heaven and earth?
Response: I believe.

Do you believe in Jesus Christ, his only Son, our Lord. He was conceived by the Holy Spirit and born of the virgin Mary. He suffered under Pontius Pilate, was crucified, died and was buried. He descended into hell. On the third day he rose again. He ascended into heaven, and is seated at the right hand of the Father. He will come again to judge the living and the dead?
Response: I believe.

Do you believe in the Holy Spirit, the holy Christian church, the communion of saints, the forgiveness of sins, the resurrection of the body and the life everlasting?
Response: I believe.

Receive the sign of the cross, on your head and on your heart, as a sign that you will know the Lord, the power of his resurrection, and the fellowship of his suffering.

_____*Name*_____, I baptize you in the name of the Father, and of the ✢ Son, and of the Holy Spirit. Amen.

Almighty God, the Father of our Lord Jesus Christ, who has given you the new birth by water and the Holy Spirit and forgiven you all your sins, strengthen you with his grace for life eternal. Amen.

Peace be with you.

Let us pray.
Almighty and merciful God and Father, we give you thanks for preserving and extending your church and for granting _____*Name*_____ the new birth in Holy Baptism, receiving *him/her* as your child and an heir to your eternal kingdom. We humbly ask you to defend and keep *him/her* in this grace, that *he/she* may never depart from you, but may always live according to your will, finally receiving the fullness of your promise in your eternal kingdom, through Jesus Christ your Son our Lord, who lives and reigns with you and the Holy Spirit, ever one God, world without end. Amen.

For the baptism of children.

Dear Christian friends:
As sponsors you are witnesses that this child has been baptized in the name of the Father, and of the Son, and of the Holy Spirit. You are also to remember *him/her* before God in prayer; and, if the parents are not able to fulfill their obligations, you shall, as far as possible, see to it that the Holy Scriptures are placed in *his/her* hands, that *he/she* is taught the Ten Commandments, the Creed and the Lord's Prayer, and that *he/she* is brought to the services of God's house, so that as *he/she* grows in years *he/she* may abide in Christ, even as now, through Holy Baptism, *he/she* has been grafted into him.

The blessing of Almighty God, the Father, the ✢ Son, and the Holy Spirit, be with you always. Amen.

A hymn may be sung.

ORDER FOR HOLY BAPTISM

EMERGENCY BAPTISM

When an unbaptized child is in danger of dying, and no pastor is available, any Christian should proceed to administer the Sacrament of Holy Baptism.

Apply water to the head of the child saying:

I baptize you in the name of the Father, and of the ✢ Son, and of the Holy Spirit. Amen.

If time allows, the Lord's Prayer may be said.

In the case of an adult, ask:

Do you believe in Jesus Christ?

Do you wish to be baptized?

Upon affirmation proceed to apply water to the person's head saying:

I baptize you in the name of the Father, and of the ✢ Son, and of the Holy Spirit. Amen.

If time allows, the Lord's Prayer may be said.

The baptism should be reported to the home congregation.

Order for a Wedding

Music appropriate for a Christian service may be inserted wherever fitting.

In the name of the Father, and of the ✟ Son, and of the Holy Spirit. Amen.

Dearly beloved, we are gathered together here in the sight of God and in the presence of this company to unite this man and this woman in holy matrimony, which is an estate instituted by God, and signifies for us the mystical union between Christ and his church, and therefore not to be entered lightly, but with reverence for God and for one another.

An appropriate text is read followed by a sermon.

Let us hear the Word of the Lord concerning this estate.

Our Lord Jesus Christ said, "Have you not read that he who created them from the beginning made them male and female and said, 'Therefore a man shall leave his father and his mother and hold fast to his wife, and they shall become one flesh'? So they are no longer two but one flesh" (Matthew 19:4-6a).

Remember also that the same Jesus Christ our Lord, when he was invited to the wedding in Cana of Galilee, gladly came and sat at table with the bridegroom and the bride, and revealed his glory, and blessed them. Invite the Lord likewise to be your guest, and pray that he may abide with you, and you with him, in his word and in his church. And the Lord will make known his glory to you, so that you will be strong in faith, sanctified in truth, and guarded from evil.

And although, by reason of sin, many a cross has been laid upon this estate, nevertheless our gracious Father in heaven does not forsake his children in an estate so holy and acceptable to him, but is ever present with his bountiful blessings.

Take to heart also these words of our Lord, "A new commandment I give to you, that you love one another: just as I have loved you, you also are to love one another" (John 13:34).

And further, "Whoever would be great among you must be your servant" (Matthew 20:26). For all who enter into marriage are above all to love and serve one another.

ORDER FOR A WEDDING

Be of one heart, but also of one mind. Give in neither to anger nor resentment, but pray with and for each other. Bear each other's burdens, with Christ as your example. Share mutually the trials of the day, but above all, endeavor to help one another on the way to life eternal. And the peace of God, which passes all understanding, will sanctify you in body, mind, and soul, and sustain you until the coming of our Lord and Savior, Jesus Christ.

I ask you ____*Groom's Christian Name*____, do you take this woman to be your wife, to live together according to God's holy word as husband and wife? Do you promise to love her, comfort her, honor, and keep her in sickness and in health; and forsaking all others, give yourself only to her, as long as you both shall live?

Response: I do.

I ask you ____*Bride's Christian Name*____, do you take this man to be your husband, to live together according to God's holy word as husband and wife? Do you promise to love him, comfort him, honor, and keep him in sickness and in health; and forsaking all others, give yourself only to him, as long as you both shall live?

Response: I do.

Please join hands and repeat after me.

Each repeats the vow following the minister.

I take you to be my wife/husband,
to have and to hold from this day forward,
for better for worse, for richer for poorer,
in sickness and in health,
to love and to cherish till death us do part,
according to God's holy word;
therefore, I make this solemn vow.

____*Name*____ and ____*Name*____ by their promises before God and before this assembly have joined themselves to each other as husband and wife.

Those whom God has joined together let no one put asunder. Amen.

The bride and groom exchange rings with these words.

I give you this ring as a sign of my love and faithfulness.

HYMN

The couple kneels.

The minister places his hands on their heads and prays.

Gracious God and Father: Grant your blessing to this man and this woman in their life together. Fulfill in them your love that they may be one. Strengthen them with the power of your Holy Spirit, that in both carefree and troublesome days, they may put their trust in you alone, and in your Word; and by mutual love and help fulfill the promises they have made to each other. And bring them at last to eternal life, through Jesus Christ our Lord. **Amen.**

LORD'S PRAYER

Our Father, who art in heaven,
   hallowed by thy name,
   thy kingdom come,
   thy will be done,
      on earth as it is in heaven.
Give us this day our daily bread;
and forgive us our trespasses,
   as we forgive those
      who trespass against us;
and lead us not into temptation,
   but deliver us from evil.
For thine is the kingdom,
   and the power, and the glory,
   forever and ever. Amen.

The couple rises.

BENEDICTION

The Lord bless you, and keep you,
The Lord make his face shine upon you, and be gracious unto you.
The Lord lift up his countenance upon you, and ✠ give you peace.

Amen.

Order for a Funeral

Stand

Processional

A funeral pall may be used. A hymn may be sung.

In the name of the Father, and of the ✛ Son, and the Holy Spirit. Amen.

Repeat after me:

Lord have mercy.
Lord have mercy.

Christ have mercy.
Christ have mercy.

Lord have mercy.
Lord have mercy.

Let us pray.

Instead of Psalm 130, a brief prayer may be said.

> Out of the depths I cry to you, O Lord!
>   O Lord, hear my voice!
> Let your ears be attentive
>   to the voice of my pleas for mercy!
> If you, O Lord, should mark iniquities,
>   O Lord, who could stand?
> But with you there is forgiveness,
>   that you may be feared.
> I wait for the Lord, my soul waits,
>   and in his word do I hope;
> my soul waits for the Lord
>   more than watchmen for the morning,
>   more than watchmen for the morning.
> O Israel, hope in the Lord!
>   For with the Lord there is steadfast love,
>   and with him is plentiful redemption.
> And he will redeem Israel from all his iniquities (Psalm 130).
> **Amen.**

Sit

THE "WAY OF SALVATION" TEXTS

The Lord is my shepherd;
>I shall not want.
>He makes me lie down in green pastures.
>>He leads me besides still waters.
>>He restores my soul.
>He leads me in paths of righteousness,
>>for his name's sake.
>Even though I walk through the valley of the shadow of death,
>>I will fear no evil, for you are with me;
>>your rod and your staff they comfort me.
>You prepare a table before me in the presence of my enemies;
>>you anoint my head with oil;
>>my cup overflows.
>Surely goodness and mercy shall follow me all the days of my life,
>>and I shall dwell in the house of the Lord forever (Psalm 23).

Dear friends, let us hear what the Holy Scriptures testify concerning the way of salvation.

>Before the mountains were brought forth,
>>or ever you had formed the earth and the world,
>>from everlasting to everlasting you are God.
>You return man to dust and say, "Return, O children of man!"
>For a thousand years in your sight are but as yesterday
>>when it is past, or as a watch in the night.
>You sweep them away as with a flood; they are like a dream,
>>like grass that is renewed in the morning:
>in the morning it flourishes and is renewed;
>>in the evening it fades and withers.
>So teach us to number our days
>>that we may get a heart of wisdom (Psalm 90:2-6, 12).

And furthermore it is written:
>"Sin came into the world through one man, and death through sin, and so death spread to all men because all sinned" (Romans 5:12).

>"Each person is destined to die once and after that comes judgment" (see Hebrews 9:27).

Let us also hear about the watchfulness and preparedness which the Lord desires to find in us.

> "Be on guard, keep awake. For you do not know when the time will come. It is like a man going on a journey, when he leaves home and puts his servants in charge, each with his work, and commands the doorkeeper to stay awake. Therefore stay awake—for you do not know when the master of the house will come, in the evening, or at midnight, or when the cock crows, or in the morning—lest he come suddenly and find you asleep. And that is what I say to all: Stay awake" (Mark 13:33-37).

Finally let us hear the blessed words concerning resurrection and everlasting life.

> "I am the resurrection and the life. Whoever believes in me, though he die, yet shall he live, and everyone who lives and believes in me shall never die" (John 11:25-26).

And the Apostle Paul writes, "For this perishable body must put on the imperishable, and this mortal must put on immortality. When the perishable puts on the imperishable, and the mortal puts on immortality, then shall come to pass the saying that is written:

> 'Death is swallowed up in victory!'
> 'O death, where is your victory?
>   O death where is your sting?'

But thanks be to God who gives us the victory through our Lord Jesus Christ" (1 Corinthians 15:53-55, 57).

The word of the Lord.

If the above "Way of Salvation" texts are not used, an appropriate selection from the following may be used.

ALTERNATE SCRIPTURE TEXTS

> "So we do not lose heart. Though our outer nature is wasting away, our inner nature is being renewed day by day. For this slight momentary affliction is preparing for us an eternal weight of glory beyond all comparison, as we look not to the things that are seen but to the things that are unseen. For the things that are seen are transient, but the things that are unseen are eternal" (2 Corinthians 4:16-18).

– OR –

"Truly, truly, I say to you, whoever hears my word and believes him who sent me has eternal life. He does not come into judgment, but has passed from death to life" (John 5:24).

– OR –

And I heard a loud voice from the throne saying, "Behold, the dwelling place of God is with man. He will dwell with them and they will be his people, and God himself will be with them as their God. He will wipe away every tear from their eyes, and death shall be no more, neither shall there be mourning nor crying nor pain anymore, for the former things have passed away."

And he who was seated on the throne said, "Behold, I am making all things new" (Revelation 21:3-5).

The following text may be used for the burial of children.

And they were bringing children to him that he might touch them, and the disciples rebuked them. But when Jesus saw it, he was indignant and said to them, "Let the children come to me; do not hinder them, for to such belongs the kingdom of God. Truly I say to you, whoever does not receive the kingdom of God like a child shall not enter it." And he took them in his arms and blessed them, laying his hands on them (Mark 10:13-16).

Additional texts to consider:
Romans 8:31-39
1 Corinthians 15:12-26
1 Peter 1:3-9
Revelation 7:9-17
John 11:21-27
John 14:1-10

Obituary may be read.

Eulogy may be included.

HYMN OR SOLO

Stand

LESSON

The Lesson is written in the _____ chapter of _____ .

After the Lesson the reader may say, "The word of the Lord."

Sit

SERMON

The sermon ends with the Nunc Dimittis, which may be said or sung (see Hymn 17).

NUNC DIMITTIS

Lord, now let your servant depart in peace,
   according to your word.
For my eyes have seen your salvation,
   which you have prepared before the face of all people:
A light to lighten the Gentiles
   and the glory of your people Israel.
Glory be to the Father, and to the Son,
   and to the Holy Spirit,
As it was in the beginning, is now, and ever shall be,
   world without end. Amen.

HYMN

PRAYER

One of the following prayers may be said, followed by the Lord's Prayer.

Let us pray.
Merciful and everlasting God, who by the death of your Son has removed from us the doom of eternal death, and has sanctified the grave to your faithful people, so that it has become a peaceful resting place, help us to be diligently mindful of our last hour, so that by true repentance and faith we may die daily to sin and to the corruptible ways of this world, and together with all your saints, be raised up daily to eternal life, through your Son, Jesus Christ our Lord. Amen.

—OR—

Gracious Father, through Jesus Christ, your Word made flesh, you have given us abundant comfort against death. Comfort us now by your Word and Holy Spirit, that we be not turned away from you by any distress, or assault of evil, but rather live in the hope you have given us, and depart this life in your peace, and in your keeping rest, until we are raised by your power to join the redeemed where sin and death are no more, through your Son, Jesus Christ our Lord. Amen.

— OR —

O God, our heavenly Father, to whom can we turn for help? Only you can heal the broken hearted and bind up their wounds. Have compassion on your servants whose joy has been turned to sorrow. Do not leave them without comfort. Rather let this sorrow draw them closer to you and to one another. Fill their lives with your presence and with a vision of that life where all mysteries will be revealed and all tears wiped away, that they may be able to abide, until that morning breaks when all darkness flees; though Jesus Christ our Lord. Amen.

Other prayers may be said.

THE LORD'S PRAYER

Our Father, who art in heaven,
 hallowed by thy name,
 thy kingdom come,
 thy will be done,
  on earth as it is in heaven.
Give us this day our daily bread;
and forgive us our trespasses,
 as we forgive those
  who trespass against us;
and lead us not into temptation,
 but deliver us from evil.
For thine is the kingdom,
 and the power, and the glory,
 forever and ever. Amen.

BENEDICTION

The Lord bless you, and keep you,
The Lord make his face shine upon you, and be gracious unto you.
The Lord lift up his countenance upon you, and ✢ give you peace. Amen.

HYMN

ORDER FOR A FUNERAL

GRAVESIDE COMMITTAL

A hymn may be sung.

In the name of the Father, and of the ✝ Son, and of the Holy Spirit. Amen.

> And I heard a voice from heaven saying, "Write this: Blessed are the dead who die in the Lord from now on." "Blessed indeed," says the Spirit, "that they may rest from their labors" (Revelation 14:13).
>
> "I am the resurrection and the life," says the Lord. "Whoever believes in me, though he die, yet shall he live, and everyone who lives and believes in me shall never die" (John 11:25-26).
>
> I know that my Redeemer lives, and at the last he will stand upon the earth. And after my skin has been thus destroyed, yet in my flesh I shall see God (Job 19:25).

In the sure and certain hope of resurrection to eternal life through Jesus Christ our Lord, we commit _____Name's_____ body to the ground: earth to earth, ashes to ashes, dust to dust.

Earth may be cast upon the coffin three times saying:

Out of dust you were taken.
Unto dust you shall return.
Out of the dust you will rise again.

> Blessed be the God and Father of our Lord Jesus Christ! According to his great mercy, he has caused us to be born again to a living hope through the resurrection of Jesus Christ from the dead (1 Peter 1:3).

At the burial of a child.

> O God, whose dear Son took little children into his arms and blessed them; with confidence in your grace we now leave this child in your hands, praying that we may all come at last to your heavenly kingdom through your Son, Jesus Christ our Lord. Amen.

O Lord, who by your death did take away the sting of death: Grant to us your servants so to follow in faith where you have led the way, that we may fall peacefully asleep in you, and awake in your likeness, through your mercy, O Lord, for you live and reign with the Father and the Holy Spirit, one God, now and forever. Amen.

THE LORD'S PRAYER

Our Father, who art in heaven,
   hallowed by thy name,
   thy kingdom come,
   thy will be done,
      on earth as it is in heaven.
Give us this day our daily bread;
and forgive us our trespasses,
   as we forgive those
      who trespass against us;
and lead us not into temptation,
   but deliver us from evil.
For thine is the kingdom,
   and the power, and the glory,
      forever and ever. Amen.

The grace of our Lord Jesus Christ, the love of God, and the fellowship of the Holy Spirit be with you all.

✠

PSALM 149:1
✠
PSALM 119:89

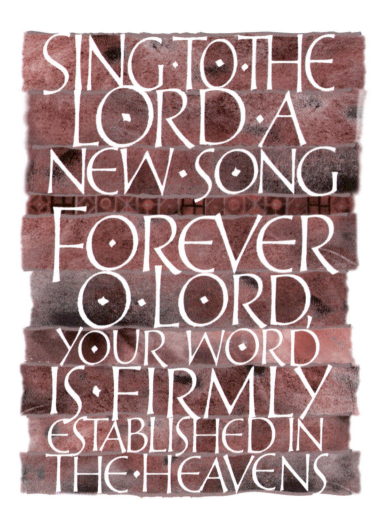

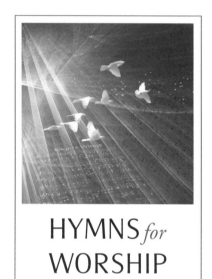

HYMNS *for* WORSHIP

© Text: Jack Hayford Copyright © 1981 New Spring (ASCAP)
© Tune: Jack Hayford. Copyright © 1981 New Spring (ASCAP)

MAJESTY
9 12 9 12 12 12 9 12

Written by Hayford while in England during the twenty-fifth anniversary of Queen Elizabeth when he realized that true majesty existed in Christ, not in earthly royalty.

Text: John Ylvisaker, b. 1937, © 1985 John C. Ylvisaker
Tune: John Ylvisaker, b. 1937, © 1985 John C. Ylvisaker

WATERLIFE
97 96 D

John Ylvisaker wrote this hymn for a baptism to show how the baptismal promises follow us through life.

TRUST, CONFIDENCE

6

Psalm 90:1

O God, Our Help in Ages Past

1. O God, our help in ages past, Our hope for years to come,
Our shelter from the storm-y blast, And our eternal home:

2. Under the shadow of your throne Your saints have dwelt secure;
Sufficient is your arm alone, And our defense is sure.

3. Before the hills in order stood Or earth received its frame,
From everlasting you are God, To endless years the same.

4. A thousand ages in your sight Are like an evening gone,
Short as the watch that ends the night Before the rising sun.

5. Time, like an ever-rolling stream,
Soon bears us all away;
We fly forgotten, as a dream
Dies at the op'ning day.

6. O God, our help in ages past,
Our hope for years to come,
Still be our guard while troubles last
And our eternal home!

Text: Isaac Watts, 1674–1748, alt.
Tune: William Croft, 1678–1727
Isaac Watts, the son of a Non-Conformist English pastor, wrote many hymns based on the Psalms.
This popular English hymn is considered to be one of his greatest.

ST. ANNE
CM

COMMUNION
8

Just as I Am, Without One Plea

John 6:37

1. Just as I am, without one plea, But that thy blood was shed for me, And that thou bidd'st me come to thee, O Lamb of God, I come, I come.

2. Just as I am, and waiting not To rid my soul of one dark blot, To thee, whose blood can cleanse each spot, O Lamb of God, I come, I come.

3. Just as I am, though tossed about With many a conflict, many a doubt, Fightings and fears within, without, O Lamb of God, I come, I come.

4. Just as I am, poor, wretched, blind; Sight, riches, healing of the mind, Yea, all I need, in thee to find, O Lamb of God, I come, I come.

5. Just as I am, thou wilt receive,
   Wilt welcome, pardon, cleanse, relieve;
   Because thy promise I believe,
   O Lamb of God, I come, I come.

6. Just as I am; thy love unknown
   Has broken ev'ry barrier down;
   Now to be thine, yea, thine alone,
   O Lamb of God, I come, I come.

Text: Charlotte Elliot, 1789–1871
Tune: William B. Bradbury, 1816–1868

WOODWORTH
LM

Charlotte Elliott wrote this after a pastor told her she should come just as she was—a sinner—to Jesus who would receive her.

Ephesians 1:7-10
Amazing Grace

COMMUNION
9

1. A-maz-ing grace, how sweet the sound, That saved a wretch like me! I once was lost, but now am found; Was blind, but now I see.
2. 'Twas grace that taught my heart to fear, And grace my fears re-lieved; How pre-cious did that grace ap-pear The hour I first be-lieved!
3. Through man-y dan-gers, toils, and snares I have al-read-y come; 'Tis grace has brought me safe thus far, And grace will lead me home.
4. The Lord has prom-ised good to me; His Word my hope se-cures; He will my shield and por-tion be As long as life en-dures.

Text: John Newton, 1725–1807
Tune: W. Walker, *Southern Harmony*, 1835
John Newton, a former slave ship captain, wrote this hymn after his conversion.

NEW BRITAIN
CM

POST COMMUNION
10 *Colossians 1:12-14*
O Jesus, Blessed Lord to Thee

1 O Jesus, blessed Lord, to thee My heartfelt thanks forever be,
2 Break forth, my soul, for joy, and say: What wealth is come to me this day!

Who hast so lovingly bestowed On me thy body and thy blood.
My Savior dwells within me now: How blest am I! how good art thou!

Text: Thomas Hansen Kingo 1634–1703; tr. Arthur James Mason 1851–1928
Tune: V. Schumann, *Geistliche Lieder*, 1539

VOM HIMMEL HOCH
LM

Written by Thomas Kingo, this is a standard Danish post communion hymn of thanksgiving.

Text: Carl Boberg, 1850–1940 (Swedish); Stuart K. Hine, 1899 (English), © 1953, 1981 Manna Music, Inc.
Tune: Swedish folk tune; arr. Stuart K. Hine, 1899, © 1953, 1981 Manna Music, Inc.

O STORE GUD
11 10 11 10 and refrain

Carl Boberg, a Swedish pastor, wrote this after seeing a violent thunderstorm and then a beautiful calm.

THANKSGIVING
13
John 1
Sunshine and Rain

© Text: Britt G. Hallqvist, 1914–1997; tr. Gracia Grindal, b. 1943, © 2006 Reclaim Resources.
© Tune: Egil Hovland, b. 1934. Copyright © Norsk Musikforlag A/S, Oslo.

MÅNE OCH SOL
4 4 5 4 4 4 8 with refrain

A Laudamus for a children's service written by Sweden's most popular hymn writer, Britt G. Hallqvist, and Norway's most famous hymn tune composer, Egil Hovland.

Text: Rick Founds, b. 1954. Copyright © Maranatha Praise, Inc. ASCAP
Tune: Rick Founds, b. 1954. Copyright © Maranatha Praise, Inc. ASCAP

LIFT YOUR NAME ON HIGH
Irregular

Written after the author/composer realized the cycle of rain from the sky to the earth and back again was very much like the cycle of blessing, praise, and thanksgiving.

5 Hold thou thy cross before my closing eyes,
　Shine through the gloom, and point me to the skies;
　Heav'n's morning breaks, and earth's vain shadows flee;
　In life, in death, O Lord, abide with me.

Text: Henry F. Lyte, 1793–1847
Tune: William H. Monk, 1823–1889
Henry Lyte, an Anglican priest, wrote this not long before he preached his last sermon in 1847, shortly before he died.

EVENTIDE
10 10 10 10

Luke 2:22-40

Nunc Dimittis

CLOSING
17

Text: Paraphrase, John Ylvisaker, b. 1937, © 2000 John C. Ylvisaker
Tune: Trad. Norwegian; arr. John Ylvisaker, b. 1937, © 2000 John C. Ylvisaker
A metrical paraphrase of the Song of Simeon.

SO RO GODT BARN
866578

HYMNS *for the* CHURCH YEAR

Text: Philipp Nicolai, 1556–1608; tr. Winkworth, 1829–1878; Grindal, 1943. Copyright © 2006 Reclaim Resources
Tune: Adapted and harm. Philipp Nicolai, 1556–1608

WACHET AUF
PM

Known as the "King of Chorales," this is the work of Philipp Nicolai, a German Lutheran pastor who lived through terrible wars, famines, and plagues at the end of the sixteenth century.

Luke 2:8-12
Silent Night, Holy Night

CHRISTMAS
21

1 Silent night, holy night! All is calm, all is bright Round yon virgin mother and child. Holy Infant, so tender and mild, Sleep in heavenly peace, Sleep in heavenly peace.

2 Silent night, holy night! Shepherds quake at the sight; Glories stream from heaven afar, Heav'nly hosts . . . sing Alleluia! Christ, the Savior, is born! Christ, the Savior, is born!

3 Silent night, holy night! Son of God, love's pure light Radiant beams from your holy face, With the dawn of redeeming grace, Jesus, Lord, at your birth, Jesus, Lord, at your birth.

Text: Joseph Mohr, 1792–1849; tr. John F. Young, 1820–1885
Tune: Franz Gruber, 1787–1863

STILLE NACHT
Irregular

Franz Gruber is said to have written this tune for the guitar to Mohr's text on December 24, 1818, when the church organ failed.

EPIPHANY
22
Matthew 2:1-2
Bright and Glorious Is the Sky

1 Bright and glorious is the sky, Radiant are the heav'ns high
  Where the golden stars are shining. All their rays to earth inclining
  Beckon us to heav'n above, Beckon us to heav'n above.

2 On that holy Christmas night Through the darkness beamed a light;
  All the stars above were paling, All their luster slowly failing
  As the Christmas star drew nigh, As the Christmas star drew nigh.

3 Sages from the East afar, When they saw this wondrous star,
  Went to find the king of nations And to offer their oblations
  Unto him as Lord and King, Unto him as Lord and King.

4 Him they found in Bethlehem, Yet he wore no diadem;
  They but saw a maiden lowly With an infant pure and holy
  Resting in her loving arms, Resting in her loving arms.

5 Guided by the star, they found
   Him whose praise the ages sound.
   We too have a star to guide us
   Which forever will provide us
   With the light to find our Lord.

6 As a star, God's holy Word
   Leads us to our king and lord;
   Brightly from its sacred pages
   Shall this light throughout the ages
   Shine upon our path of life.

Text: Nikolai F. S. Grundtvig 1783–1872; tr. *Service Book and Hymnal*, © 1958
Tune: Danish, 1830

DEJLIG ER DEN HIMMEL BLAA
77 88 77

Nicolai Grundtvig's Epiphany hymn about the coming of the Wise Men to worship Jesus was written in 1810.

Galatians 6:14

In the Cross of Christ I Glory

LENT
23

1 In the cross of Christ I glory, Tow'r-ing o'er the wrecks of time. All the light of sa-cred sto-ry Gath-ers round its head sub-lime.

2 When the woes of life o'er-take me, Hopes de-ceive, and fears an-noy, Nev-er shall the cross for-sake me; Lo, it glows with peace and joy.

3 When the sun of bliss is beam-ing Light and love up-on my way, From the cross the ra-diance stream-ing Adds more lus-ter to the day.

4 Bane and bless-ing, pain and plea-sure, By the cross are sanc-ti-fied; Peace is there that knows no mea-sure, Joys that through all time a-bide.

Text: John Bowring, 1792–1872
Tune: Ithamar Conkey, 1815–1867

RATHBUN
87 87

John Bowring, a gifted linguist, may have written this hymn after seeing a bronze cross in a ruined cathedral in Macoa, China.

5 Therefore, kind Jesus, since I cannot pay thee,
 I do adore thee, and will ever pray thee;
 Think on thy pity and thy love unswerving,
 Not my deserving.

Job 19:25-30
I Know that My Redeemer Lives!

EASTER
27

1. I know that my Redeemer lives! What comfort this sweet sentence gives! He lives, he lives, who once was dead; He lives, my ever-living head!
2. He lives triumphant from the grave; He lives eternally to save; He lives exalted, throned above; He lives to rule his Church in love.
3. He lives to grant me rich supply; He lives to guide me with his eye; He lives to comfort me when faint; He lives to hear my soul's complaint.
4. He lives to silence all my fears; He lives to wipe away my tears; He lives to calm my troubled heart; He lives all blessings to impart.

5 He lives to bless me with his love;
He lives to plead for me above;
He lives my hungry soul to feed;
He lives to help in time of need.

6 He lives, my kind, wise, heav'nly friend;
He lives and loves me to the end;
He lives, and while he lives, I'll sing;
He lives, my Prophet, Priest, and King!

7 He lives and grants me daily breath;
He lives, and I shall conquer death;
He lives my mansion to prepare;
He lives to bring me safely there.

8 He lives, all glory to his name!
He lives, my Savior, still the same;
What joy this blest assurance gives;
I know that my Redeemer lives!

Text: Samuel Medley, 1738-1799, alt.
Tune: attr. John Hatton, d. 1793

DUKE STREET
LM

Samuel Medley converted after reading a sermon by Isaac Watts and became a Baptist minister. He wrote this hymn in 1775.

5 Now softly the light of Pentecost
　Is shining its beams around us,
　God's blessings for us cannot be lost.
　As brooks in the fields surround us,
　And leave in their wake the woods and fields,
　The bright summer green astounds us!

6 With joy we depart for our Father's land
　Where God with his Son is dwelling.
　A mansion is waiting, gold and grand,
　A mansion beyond excelling;
　And there we will walk in endless light
　As we all his praise are telling.

Text: Nikolai F. S. Grundtvig 1783–1872; tr. Smeby, Rygh, Døving, Grindal. Copyright © 2006 Reclaim Resources
Tune: Christoph E. F. Weyse, 1774–1842

DEN SIGNEDE DAG
98 98 98

Nicolai Grundtvig revised a medieval hymn by the same title to celebrate the one thousandth anniversary of Christianity in Denmark.

Text: Martin Luther, 1483–1546; tr. hymnal version, © 1978 Lutheran Book of Worship
Tune: Martin Luther, 1483–1546

EIN FESTE BURG
87 87 66 66 7

A hymn on Psalm 46, written by Martin Luther about 1529, after a time of great spiritual strife.

Hebrews 12:7-11

TRUST, GUIDANCE

Children of the Heavenly Father

32

Text: Caroline V. Sandell Berg, 1832–1903; tr. Ernst W. Olson, 1870–1958, © Board of Publication
Tune: Swedish folk tune

TRYGGARE KAN INGEN VARA
LM

Lina Sandell, a Swedish Lutheran pastor's daughter, wrote this hymn when she was about 17.

Text: William W. How, 1823–1897
Tune: R. Vaughan Williams, 1872–1958
SINE NOMINE
10 10 10 and alleluias
The Anglican Bishop William How intended this hymn to be used during All Saints' Day celebrations.

HYMNS *for the* CHRISTIAN LIFE

Text: Thomas O. Chisholm, 1866–1960. © 1923, renewed 1951 Hope Publishing Co.
Tune: William M. Runyan, 1870–1957. © 1923, renewed 1951 Hope Publishing Co.

FAITHFULNESS
11 10 11 10 and refrain

Thomas Obadiah Chisholm, born in a log cabin in Franklin, Kentucky, was a Methodist minister who wrote this most popular of gospel songs.

5 Yet she on earth has union
  With God, the Three in One,
  And mystic sweet communion
  With those whose rest is won.

O blessed heav'nly chorus!
Lord, save us by your grace,
That we, like saints before us,
May see you face to face.

Text: Samuel J. Stone, 1839–1900
Tune: Samuel S. Wesley, 1810–1876

AURELIA
76 76 D

Samuel John Stone, a priest in the Anglican church, wrote this hymn in 1866 based on the Apostles' Creed.

Ephesians 3:11-12
My Faith Looks Up to Thee

TRUST, GUIDANCE
38

Text: Ray Palmer, 1808–1887
Tune: Lowell Mason, 1792–1872

OLIVET
6 64 666 4

Ray Palmer wrote this hymn while yet a young man during a time of illness and discouragement.

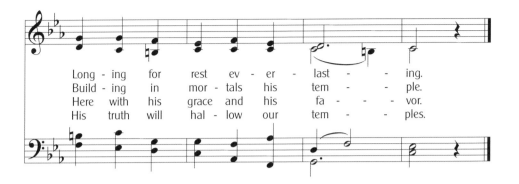

Longing for rest everlasting.
Building in mortals his temple.
Here with his grace and his favor.
His truth will hallow our temples.

5 Still we our earthly temples build
So we may herald his praises;
They are the homes his presence fills
And little children embraces,
Beautiful things in them are said,
God has in them his promise made,
Making us heirs of his kingdom.

6 Here stands the font before our eyes
Telling how God has received us;
Here we recall Christ's sacrifice
And what his table does give us;
Here sounds the word that still proclaims
Christ yesterday, today the same,
Always and now our Redeemer.

7 Grant, then, O God, where'er we live,
That, when the church-bells are ringing
Many will faith in Christ receive
Where he his message is bringing.
"I know my own, my own know me;
You, not the world, my face shall see.
My peace I leave with you." Amen.

Text: Nicolai F. S. Grundtvig 1783–1872; tr. Carl Døving; Gracia Grindal, © 2006 Reclaim Resources.
Tune: Ludvig M. Lindeman, 1812–1887

KIRKEN DEN ER ET GAMMELT HUS
88 88 88 8

Nicolai Grundtvig wrote this hymn on the church after seeing the destruction of the cathedral in Copenhagen during the British bombardment of the city in the Napoleonic Wars.

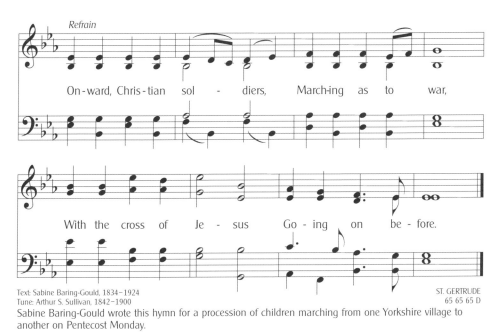

Text: Sabine Baring-Gould, 1834–1924
Tune: Arthur S. Sullivan, 1842–1900

ST. GERTRUDE
65 65 65 D

Sabine Baring-Gould wrote this hymn for a procession of children marching from one Yorkshire village to another on Pentecost Monday.

Luke 22:32

TRUST, GUIDANCE

Lord, Keep Us Steadfast in Your Word
41

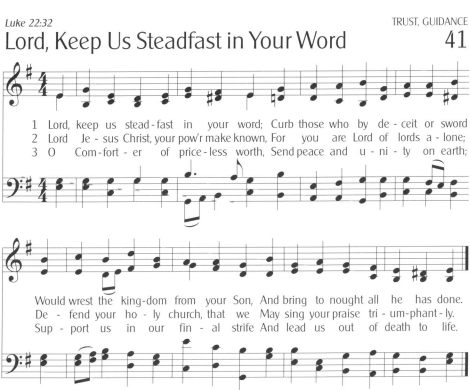

1 Lord, keep us steadfast in your word; Curb those who by deceit or sword
Would wrest the kingdom from your Son, And bring to nought all he has done.

2 Lord Jesus Christ, your pow'r make known, For you are Lord of lords alone;
Defend your holy church, that we May sing your praise triumphantly.

3 O Comforter of priceless worth, Send peace and unity on earth;
Support us in our final strife And lead us out of death to life.

Text: Martin Luther, 1483–1546
Tune: J. Klug, *Geistliche Lieder*, 1543

ERHALT UNS, HERR
LM

Written by Martin Luther in 1542 when it looked like the Lutheran movement would be defeated by the Saladin and the Roman Catholic foes whom Luther thought had joined forces against him.

Text: Katherine Hankey, 1834–1911
Tune: William G. Fischer, 1835–1912

HANKEY
76 76 D and refrain

Katherine Hankey, born in England, the daughter of a banker, worked tirelessly with young people in the city of London.

Text: Will Lamartine Thompson, 1847–1909
Tune: Will Lamartine Thompson, 1847–1909
Will L. Thompson wrote many gospel hymns that were used by Moody and Sankey in their revivals. This was one of the most successful.

FOR YOU AND FOR ME
11 7 11 7 with refrain

Psalm 131
My God, How Wonderful Thou Art

PRAISE
45

1. My God, how wonderful thou art, Thy majesty how bright! How beautiful thy mercy seat In depths of burning light!
2. How wonderful, how beautiful The sight of thee must be— Thine endless wisdom, boundless pow'r, And awesome purity!
3. No earthly father loves like thee; No mother, e'er so mild, Bears and forbears as thou hast done With me, thy sinful child.
4. Yet I may love thee too, O Lord, Almighty as thou art, For thou hast stooped to ask of me The love of my poor heart.

5. My God, how wonderful thou art,
   Thou everlasting friend!
   On thee I stay my trusting heart
   Till faith in vision end.

6. O how I fear thee, living God!
   With deepest, tend'rest fears,
   And worship thee with trembling hope,
   And penitential tears!

Text: Frederick William Faber, 1814–1863
Tune: *Psalter*, Edinburgh, 1615

DUNDEE
CM

Frederick W Faber, disappointed with the state of the Anglican church, became a priest in the Roman Catholic church in 1846.

1 Corinthians 10:4

Rock of Ages, Cleft for Me

JUSTIFICATION
47

1 Rock of Ages, cleft for me, Let me hide myself in thee;
Let the water and the blood, From thy riven side which flowed,
Be of sin the double cure, Save me from its guilt and pow'r.

2 Not the labor of my hands Can fulfil thy law's demands;
Could my zeal no respite know, Could my tears forever flow,
All for sin could not atone; Thou must save, and thou alone.

3 Nothing in my hands I bring, Simply to thy cross I cling;
Naked, come to thee for dress, Helpless look to thee for grace;
Foul, I to the fountain fly, Wash me, Savior, or I die.

4 While I draw this fleeting breath, When my eyes shall close in death,
When I soar to worlds unknown, See thee on thy judgment throne,
Rock of Ages, cleft for me, Let me hide myself in thee.

Text: August M. Toplady, 1740-1778
Tune: Thomas Hastings, 1784-1872

TOPLADY
77 77 77

Augustus Montague Toplady wrote this hymn as the conclusion of an article supporting the notion of God's election of sinners

What Makes a Hymn Lutheran?

This question will continue to rage in our midst as long as there are Lutherans! Is a hymn Lutheran because its writer grew up as a Lutheran? Or is it Lutheran because it expresses Lutheran theology? To think that only Lutherans can write Lutheran hymns is to confuse genetics with confession. Sadly, it is easy to be a genetic Lutheran these days and not have the slightest idea about Lutheran theology.

At the beginning of the last century, Lutherans numbered more than they do today, and they argued vigorously about what a Lutheran hymn was. The debate was occasioned by the question one church leader, Paul Glasoe, posed specifically in the January 1, 1931, edition of the church paper, *The Lutheran Herald*: "Are we singing our children out of the Lutheran church?"

Some feared that by insisting on singing only from the old German and Scandinavian hymns without any engagement with the American hymnbook, their children would leave for other more evangelical and American churches.

Some thought a Lutheran hymn could only be a hymn by a Lutheran, which narrowed the number of hymns available for a Lutheran hymnal. What about those from the ecumenical church?

To their credit, others argued persuasively that it was the words that made a hymn Lutheran.

N. Astrup Larsen, a missionary in China, settled it for good by saying that any hymn that told of the unconditional love of Jesus Christ for us was Lutheran.

In other words, a hymn that preaches or assumes faith alone, grace alone, word alone, Christ alone, the cross alone is a Lutheran hymn.

LUTHERAN CONFESSIONS AND HYMNS

The Lutheran Confessions are clear on this. We read from Melanchton's "Apology to the Augsburg Confession" in which he said, "Ceremonies should be observed both so that people may learn the Scriptures and so that, admonished by the Word, they might experience faith and fear and finally even pray. For these are the purposes of the ceremonies... We also use German hymns in order that the [common] people might have something to learn that will arouse their faith and fear."

This means hymns can do more than help us preach the gospel to our neighbors. They can help us praise God and pray to him. Some of our greatest and most popular hymns by non-Lutherans do that, from "Praise to the Lord the Almighty, the King of Creation," to "Great Is Thy Faithfulness," to "On Eagle's Wings." Other favorites help us pray to God, such as Luther's "Lord, Keep Us Steadfast in Your Word," or Anglican bishop Reginald Heber's "Holy, Holy, Holy," or Taize's "Jesus Remember Me When You Come into Your Kingdom." These kinds of hymns are classics that are perfectly acceptable in Lutheran services.

We are rich in hymns from the entire ecumenical and global church. Many are much beloved by people in our Lutheran churches as well as popular around the world. We can accept them into the canon of Lutheran hymns because they preach the pure gospel of Jesus, or teach of Jesus, or pray to him in the words of Scripture.

LUTHERANS AND ECUMENICAL HYMNS

We Lutherans, whose ecumenical strategy at its best rejoices in the unity we already have in Jesus Christ, can accept these hymns with pleasure into our hymnals, as we have over the generations. When Lutherans came to America and started preparing their first English hymnal, there were no serviceable English translations of German or Scandinavian hymns. So by necessity they opened up their hymnbooks to a wide variety of great English hymns. They took in many favorite hymns by Isaac Watts and Charles Wesley, which Lutherans have sung ever since with joy.

After Catherine Winkworth in the mid-nineteenth century provided English-speaking Lutherans with a treasury of German Lutheran texts in good English, Lutherans began publishing hymnals with many more Lutheran chorales in them.

The Norwegian Evangelical Church in America in 1912 produced *The Lutheran Hymnary*, which contained mostly classic Lutheran chorales that made very few gestures toward American hymnody, although it did include classic Anglican hymns such as "Holy, Holy, Holy."

The Hymnal (1925) by Swedish Augustana was very friendly to the American songbook, including gospel hymns such as "In the Sweet Bye and Bye," which enriched us.

LUTHERANS AND CONTEMPORARY HYMNS

We should continue including new hymns as well as old ones by our Christian brothers and sisters around the world, hymns that teach us how to preach, praise, and pray to Christ alone. We should not take them, however, just because they come from the global church.

Some contemporary hymns are not Lutheran hymns because they do not preach or assume the Lutheran theological fundamentals. To some, the idea that a hymn has to fit theological norms can be repellent. There are hymn writers who want to be as ignorant of theology as they can be. Their reasoning is because it brings division. The truth, however, causes divisions, and there is much strife involved in defending the faith.

Not every hymn or spiritual song written today preaches the gospel. Hymns that tell God what we are doing, and seem to imply that our works should do anything to win us favor with God, should be banned no matter where they come from or how popular they are. As the old spiritual says, "Give me Jesus." That's the main thing.

Gracia Grindal

Editor-in-Chief

A Note on the Liturgical Songs

With regard to the liturgical songs, an attempt has been made to create or select tunes that sound good played in a variety of styles and with a variety of instruments. Melody is spaceless and timeless. It is the rhythm that gives it cultural identity. These melodies can be played on the organ in a formal setting. They can also be accompanied by piano, guitars, and percussion in a less formal setting.

John Ylvisaker

Informal Service

While the idea of an order for an informal service may seem like a contradiction in terms, some things are self-evident as Martin Luther in his introduction to his German Mass noted. "Center everything on the Word, prayer, and love." The following is a typical order of service from Lutheran hymnals from the past. These are simply suggestions for an order, but evangelical freedom is to be used at all times.

> Invocation
> Hymn
> Scripture reading
> Prayer
> Catechism
>   The Ten Commandments
>   Creed
>   The Lord's Prayer
> Hymn
> Sermon
> Hymn
> Offering
> Hymn
> The Lord's Supper, if desired
> The Lord's Prayer
> Benediction

Acknowledgments

Luther's Small Catechism and the liturgical material, pages 6-51, are covered by the copyright of this book.

Material from the following sources is acknowledged

Scripture and Creeds
Unless otherwise indicated, all Scripture quotations are from *The Holy Bible, English Standard Version,* copyright © 2001 by Crossways Bibles, a division of Good News Publishers. Used by permission. All rights reserved.

English translations of the Apostles' Creed (adapted) and Nicene Creed (adapted) © English Language Liturgical Consultation (ELLC), 1988, and used by permission. See: www.englishtexts.org

Liturgical Music
The composer of the Saint Paul's Setting is John C. Ylvisaker (b. 1937).

Kyrie Eleison
  Text: Traditional
  Tune: WILSHIRE COURT, © 2006 John C. Ylvisaker.
Gloria in Excelsis
  Text: Paraphrase, © 2006 John C. Ylvisaker
  Tune: WESLEY CHAPEL, © 2006 John C. Ylvisaker
Hallelu, Hallelujah
  Text: © 2006 John C. Ylvisaker
  Tune: Trad. American, BELLEVUE
Lenten Sentence
  Text: © 2000 John C. Ylvisaker
  Tune: Trad. American Shaker, CARNAL LIFE, arr. John C. Ylvisaker, © 2000
Sanctus
  Text: Traditional
  Tune: WILSHIRE COURT, © 2006 John C. Ylvisaker
Agnus Dei
  Text: Paraphrase, John C. Ylvisaker, © 2006
  Tune: HANLEY AVENUE, John C. Ylvisaker, © 2006
Aaron's Benediction
  Text: Numbers 6 paraphrase, John C. Ylvisaker, © 1990
  Tune: Trad. South African, BRANDY, arr. John C. Ylvisaker © 1990

Liturgical Texts and the Small Catechism
Authors and translators are: Gracia Grindal, Scott Grorud, M. Luther Johnson, Lawrence J. Lystig, Norman P. Olsen, Oliver K. Olson.

Proofreaders
We gratefully acknowledge: Mary Ellen Amundson, Clarice Dieter, Jerrold Itzen, Minette Johnson, Paul Johnson, Ruth Moerke, Ramona Olsen, and Donald Rosholt.

Reclaim Resources Committee Members
Bob Amundson, treasurer; Gracia Grindal, editor-in-chief; Scott Grorud; M. Luther Johnson, administrative co-chair; Sarah Johnson, secretary; Carolyn Lystig, managing editor; Norman P. Olsen; Oliver K. Olson; Rosalie Rosholt, administrative co-chair. Advisory members are: Darla Bielfeldt, Roy A. Harrisville, Tom Maakestad, Walter Sundberg, and Former Minnesota Governor Al Quie.

Music Engraving
Paul Gerike, Music Advantage, 112328 Chatfield Ct. Chaska, Minn. 55318 (952) 448-7544

Logo Design and Publisher
Koechel Peterson and Associates, Minneapolis, Minn., and Reclaim Resources in cooperation with Bronze Bow Publishing, Minneapolis, Minn.

Copyrights and Permissions
Reclaim Resources gratefully acknowledges all the copyright owners for granting permission to reproduce their material in this book.

Every effort has been made to contact the copyright holders and/or the administrators for each of the copyrighted material for permission to reprint. The publishers, upon written notice, will make necessary corrections in subsequent printings.

Permission Information
Permission to reproduce any of the copyrighted material in this book must be obtained from the copyright holders of that material. See the next page for copyright information.

Thank you for your gifts
The Reclaim hymnal project is being subsidized by gifts from many individuals, households, and groups. We are a non-profit organization and invite your donations. *Please send to:*

Reclaim Resources
PO Box 8202
Saint Paul, MN 55108
800-590-6001
www.ReclaimLutheranWorship.org

Copyright Information

31 "A Mighty Fortress Is Our God." Copyright ©1978 *Lutheran Book of Worship*. Used by permission of Augsburg Fortress.

22 "Bright and Glorious Is the Sky." Text copyright ©1958 *Service Book and Hymnal*. Used by permission of Augsburg Fortress.

39 "Built on the Rock." Text copyright ©2006 Reclaim Resources. All rights reserved.

32 "Children of the Heavenly Father." Text copyright © Board of Publication, Lutheran Church in America. Used by permission of Augsburg Fortress.

36 "Great Is Thy Faithfulness." Copyright ©1923. Renewed 1951. Hope Publishing Co., Carol Stream, Illinois. Used with permission.

12 "How Great Thou Art." Copyright ©1953 S. K. Hine. Assigned to Manna Music, Inc., 35255 Brooten Road, Pacific City, Oregon 97135. Renewed 1981 by Manna Music, Inc. All rights reserved. Used by permission. (ASCAP)

5 "I Was There to Hear Your Borning Cry." Used by permission. Copyright ©1985 John C. Ylvisaker, Box 321, Waverly, Iowa 50677. (319) 352-4396

15 "Lord, I Lift Your Name on High" by Rick Founds. Copyright ©1989 Maranatha Praise, Inc./ASCAP (Administered by Music Services). All rights reserved. Used by permission.

2 "Majesty" by Jack Hayford ©1981 New Spring (ASCAP) Publishers All rights in the US administered by New Spring (ASCAP). Used by permission.

7 "Nicene Creed." Text paraphrase; tune trad. American, arr. John C. Ylvisaker. Copyright ©2006 John C. Ylvisaker. Used by permission.

17 "Nunc Dimittis." Text paraphrase; tune trad. Norwegian, arr. John C. Ylvisaker. Copyright ©2006 John C. Ylvisaker. Used by permission.

30 "O Day Full of Grace." Text copyright ©2006 Reclaim Resources. All rights reserved.

35 "On Eagle's Wings" by Michael Joncas. Copyright ©1979, OCP Publications, 5536 NE Hassalo, Portland, Oregon 97213. All rights reserved. Used with permission.

13 "Sunshine and Rain." Copyright © Norsk Musikforlag A/S, Oslo, Norway. Used by permission. English translation © 2006 Reclaim Resources.

19 "Wake, Awake for Night Is Flying." Text copyright ©2006 Reclaim Resources. All rights reserved.

Copyright Holders and Administrators

Augsburg Fortress
426 S. 5th Street,
PO Box 1209
Minneapolis, MN 55440
800-328-4648

BMG Music Publishing
8750 Wilshire Blvd., Second Floor
Beverly Hills, CA 90211
310-358-4701

Hope Publishing Company
380 South Main Place
Carol Stream, IL 60188
800-323-1049

Manna Music
PO Box 218
Pacific City, OR 97135
503-965-6112

Music Advantage
Paul Gerike
112328 Chatfield Court
Chaska, MN 55318
pgerike@mn.rr.com
952-448-7544

Music Services
1526 Otter Creek Rd,
Nashville, TN 37215
615-371-1320

New Generation Publishers
John Ylvisaker
PO Box 321
Waverly, IA 50677
319-352-4396

Norsk Musikforlag A/S
PO Box 1499 - Vika
NO - 0116 Oslo
Norway

OCP Publications
5536 NE Hassalo
Portland, OR 97213
800-548-8749

Reclaim Resources
PO Box 8202
Saint Paul, MN 55108
www.ReclaimLutheranWorship.org
800-590-6001

First Lines and Common Titles

31 A mighty fortress is our God
16 Abide with me
26 Ah, holy Jesus, how hast thou offended
 9 Amazing grace

18 Beautiful Savior
25 Beneath the cross of Jesus
 5 Borning Cry
22 Bright and glorious is the sky
39 Built on the Rock

32 Children of the heavenly Father
28 Christ the Lord is ris'n today!

33 For all the saints

46 God's word is our great heritage
36 Great is thy faithfulness

 3 Holy, holy, holy
12 How Great Thou Art

27 I know that my Redeemer lives!
34 I am weak, but thou art strong
42 I love to tell the story
 5 I was there to hear your borning cry
23 In the cross of Christ I glory

20 Joy to the world
34 Just a Closer Walk with Thee
 8 Just as I am, without one plea

15 Lord, I lift your name on high
41 Lord, keep us steadfast in your word
17 Lord, now let your servants depart
11 Lord, with grateful hearts

 2 Majesty
38 My faith looks up to thee
45 My God, how wonderful thou art
29 My hope is built on nothing less

 7 Nicene Creed
14 Now thank we all our God
17 Nunc Dimittis

30 O day full of grace
 6 O God, our help in ages past
10 O Jesus, blessed Lord to thee
12 O Lord my God, when I in awesome wonder
24 O sacred head, now wounded
35 On Eagle's Wings
40 Onward Christian soldiers

 1 Praise to the Lord, the Almighty

47 Rock of Ages, cleft for me

44 Shall we gather at the river
21 Silent night, holy night
43 Softly and tenderly Jesus is calling
13 Sunshine and rain

37 The church's one foundation

19 Wake, awake, for night is flying
 7 We believe in the Creator, God
 4 What a friend we have in Jesus

35 You, who dwell in the shelter of the Lord

A complete and permanent hymnal resource in **printed hardcover** and **electronic formats** is being created by Reclaim Resources. Included will be 4 to 6 musical settings for the service with holy communion; orders for baptism, wedding, and funeral; approximately 600 hymns; a contemporary worship planning resource; and the Augsburg Confession and Luther's Small Catechism.

For more information, call 800.590.6001 or visit www.ReclaimLutheranWorship.org.